# Prayers
# In the
# 2020s

by
Ashton S. Dupler
&
Edward K. Solano Johnson

DSM

Published by DSM Story Forge

ISBN: 979-8-9861562-8-6 (Paperback)
ISBN: 979-8-9861562-9-3 (eBook)

Any references to historical events, real people, or real places are used fictitiously. Names, characters, and places are products of the author's imagination.

Published by DSM Story Forge, LLC in the United States of America.

First printing edition 2023.

DSM Story Forge
1733 Boulder Court
Powell, OH
43065

www.dsmstoryforge.com

# Table of Contents

# **Foreword**

Genuine prayer is the most honest of spaces. It is the experience of unguarded communion, an incomprehensible and yet fully accessible act of simply being with God. Standing before God, with nothing hidden or tucked away, we are fully known. Perhaps this is the reason we so often resist the life of prayer, for the thought of being fully known ignites the fear and insecurity within. To be known is to be exposed, and to be exposed is to face rejection. Fearful of being seen, we hide behind prayers that are safe and appropriate, talking to God in pious language that will not betray our true thoughts and feelings.

But safe and perfunctory prayer is not the prayer of the Psalmist, the prophets, or of Jesus. The prayer we see modeled in Scripture is nothing if not honest, perhaps too honest at times for our religious sensibilities. It is a place of communion with God, so real and genuine, that there is also room to wrestle with God. The nagging questions we keep tamped down below the surface are welcome in this place. Our painful struggles with fear, loneliness, worry, and even vengeance, can be given voice. Perhaps surprisingly, the recorded prayers of Scripture also show us that such ruthless honesty does not bring us rejection at all. To the contrary, it opens the door to an encounter with God that deepens our trust and renews our hope. In our willingness to be fully known, we discover that we are fully loved. And
not only are we loved, but this God who loves us is faithfully with us, even in the broken places.

These are days that call for honest prayer. The unprecedented has become commonplace with one unexpected and unwanted challenge piling on top of another. Fear and uncertainty govern our lives, spilling over into anger, blame, and judgment. We have withdrawn into circles of isolation, desperately trying to find some sense of security, some way to get control over the chaos around us. What we need is a place to pour out the fear welling up inside us, the questions and uncertainties that haunt us, and the anger we so easily allow to drive us. We need to pray, but not the safe and pious prayers that deny our reality. We need to honestly pray.

Ashton Dupler and Edward Solano, in this collection of prayers, help us to put into practice the genuine act of prayer that we so desperately need. They will help you find words for circumstances that seem beyond words, guiding you toward a prayer room of communion with God that is wholly, unapologetically honest. Know going in that to pray this way is to be fully known. What you will discover through these prayers, however, is that you are also fully loved by a God who is faithfully present.

Douglas Van Nest

Dean of the School of Christian Ministry and
Professor of Christian Ministry
at Mount Vernon Nazarene University

# **Introduction**

"Prayer Changes Things," read the sign that hung in one of our college study rooms. We could never understand why that statement felt empty, at least until this past couple years. It would be hard to find someone who was left untouched by the COVID-19 pandemic that has killed over a million people in the USA. Prayers during the uncertainties of the last three years were not simply to change things; they were the sad, anxious attempts to express the aching of our hearts. We lifted up sick friends and family, prayed for our sense of loneliness, and dealt with our own anxiety. The great pastor and theologian Howard Thurman states that "a man prays for loved ones because he has to, not merely because his prayers may accomplish something beyond this." But, one might ask, what is there beyond praying as a way to plead for the accomplishment of our hearts desire? We think that one can pray as a desperate means of survival, an overflow of the heart in the face of a multiplying crisis. We think there is prayer that simply exists, like the air necessary to breath when one faces uncertain situations. We think that there are prayers that are just "prayed" when history unfolds with years like 2020, 2021, 2022, and so on. It is a way of praying that simply "is." Prayers that God uses to change things in our lives when they are simply "prayed".

For each of us writing this book, prayer simply "is." It is not a tool or even a goal, but it is the cry of our hearts. We wrote this "book of prayers" because we desired to pray together, to lift each other up, and lift up our concerns to the One who cares. We often call up friends to vent about all kinds of situations; none of these they can change, but they hold our hearts together as we wrestle with anger, hope, disappointment, every-day joys and difficulties. God can change situations, and in the last few years we have definitely called on our Lord to vent about many things. The last few years we have heard prayers before peaceful protests and prayers that sanctify violence. We have seen prayers against wearing masks and prayers for masks to protect us. Prayers have been lifted for family members as they fight cancer, COVID-19, a cold, and for those left in loneliness. With all of this in mind, and from this point, is that this project was born.

Prayer is the language of both the sacred and the ordinary. When we know God, we cannot help but to lift up our situation, and not just lift it up, but also confront it. The Jewish Rabbi, Abraham Joshua Heschel said, "Prayer… is a radical commitment, a dangerous involvement in the life of God." Writing this book has shown us that true prayers are not demands that we make to God. Prayers are pleas in many forms, and different words, so that our hearts can be aligned with God's heart. In many ways, prayers ask more of us than they ask of God. For example, when we pray "your kingdom come, your will be done" we are praying for something to happen *in us*. We are not only asking for God's will and God's reign to come to this world, we plead for God to work *in us*.

Praying the statement "your kingdom come, your will be done" demands more from us than it does from God. God has already sent the Son (Jn. 3:16), and God has already revealed God's creative hand through creation (Gen. 1-2; Rom. 1:20). But it is still necessary for us to choose worshiping on a daily basis. It is *I* (individually) and *we* (communally) who must choose God with all we do, so that the Father's kingdom can come in and through our life, and so that the Father's will can be done in and through our life. This means that we need to let God do God's transformative work in our being, and for that, we need to surrender who we are to God. That is why, praying "your kingdom come, your will be done" is more demanding to us than to God. It reminds us that we need to choose God by trust in God's faithful loving presence. It challenges us to align our hearts with God's desire.

Our hope is that the next few pages do that for you, that they remind and challenge you to choose and trust in God. The book that you are about to read has 52 prayers. Each prayer is a plea about something that the world has confronted throughout the decade that started with the year 2020. The prayers have been divided in 7 sections, each section belongs to a statement in the Lord's Prayer found in the Gospel according to Matthew. We believe that each of these prayers is a plea that faithfully relates with at least one statement from the Lord's Prayer. They might even be considered contextualized depictions of the Lord's Prayer. Also, please note that many of the prayers are accompanied by an illustration: a visual depiction of a verbal prayer. Please allow these illustrations to help you reflect and pray as you read this book.

Finally, as you go through the next pages, we thank you for praying with us. Let's continue lifting our hearts to God because God cares for us and God listens to our prayers.

# Our Father, who are in heaven, hallowed be your name

*There is none holy like the Lord; there is none besides you; there is no rock like our God.*

*1 Samuel 2:2 (NIV)*

# Prayer Amidst a Pandemic

Lord, our God,
We are tired,
Tired of wearing masks,
Tired of getting vaccines,
Tired of not seeing family,
And tired of social distancing.

We thought that everything was getting better,
That the pandemic was coming to an end,
But now more cases are visible,
More deaths are declared,
There is doubt about the vaccines,
And, honestly, we feel trapped by the pandemic again.

Here and now, amidst all,
We pray to you.
We believe in you.
We trust you with our future.
We trust you with our health.
We trust you with the health of our loved ones.

We surrender our fears to you,
We lay our confusion at your feet,
We place our families in your hands,
We leave our jobs to your will,
God, all our uncertainties,
We give them to you.

We might not know what the pandemic will bring,
It might be sickness and death,
Isolation, pain, and instability,
But we know that you are here with us,
Bringing healing and life,
Your presence and your love.

We pray for your presence with us,

Your creation,
Your world,
Your people,
Your church,

Amen.

# Prayer to Make Room for God

Dear Lord,
You loved me first,
You created me, and nourished me,
You put people around me so I could grow,
You gave your life for me,
And you pursue me each day.

Today I recognize that you are worthy,
Worthy of my time,
Worthy of my days,
Worthy of the moments of my every day,
Worthy of spending one more hour with you,
And taking an hour away from Netflix.

I give you this space, this time, this moment,
Coming to you, away from all distractions.

In this room, I pray,
Please be with me.
Most beautiful Savior, right now,
I'm making room for you.
Let's talk.

Amen.

# Prayer for Setting Boundaries

Infinite God,
In a world of limitless scrolling and information,
Remind me of my limitations.
Thank you for always going before me,
Just like you did for the Israelites in the wilderness:
You have prepared good things for me.

I cast all my anxieties on to you!
I pray that I carry only what you've prepared for me,
And let the rest go.
You have given everything I need for life;
So let my "yes be yes," and my "no be no."
May I rest in your purpose.

Amen.

GOD, YOU have prepared the way for me.

Nadia Volpini

# Morning Prayer

God,
We give you thanks for this day,
Its beginning, and its foreseeable end,

Not knowing what it will bring,
Maybe joys or woes,

Even then, before it all,
We give you thanks for this day,

Praised be your name.

Amen.

# Afternoon Prayer

King Jesus,
I are at the middle of the day,
And I am exhausted.

The morning energy has worn out,
Lunch just passed by,
And I want this day to be over.

Show me your grace and your love,
Right now, in the middle of today,
I want to see you.

You who are my strength,
My ever-present help, every day,
Please, be with me this afternoon.

Amen.

# Evening Prayer

God, my rest,
I pray to you,
I thank you,
And give to you,
This day that's about to end.

I give to you,
All my joys and sorrows,
All my doubts and hopes,
All my pain, questions, thoughts,
And give you all my memories of today.

I thank you,
For the easy things,
For those difficult moments,
For the times when I felt you the closest,
And for what tomorrow will bring.

I pray for this evening's sleep,
Remind me: today is about to end,
And it is okay to close my eyes.
That tomorrow will come soon,
And, when I wake, I will still be with you.

God, tonight, help me to trust you,
To rest in you,
To let you work through my sleep,
To surrender my worries,
And find rest and peace in you.

Amen.

# Prayer Reflecting On the Gospel Of Saint John

Lord,
Remind me of your love.

Strengthen me, my God,
And I will lay down my life for others.

As I do, my Father,
Breathe your life into me.

Please, my beloved,
Transform who I am.

My Lord,
Make me more like you.

In your name I pray,
Amen.

# Your kingdom come; your will be done on earth as it is in heaven.

*The Lord will be king over the whole earth. On that day there will be one Lord, and his name the only name.*
*Zechariah 14:9 (NIV)*

# Prayer for My Dreams and Goals

God,
I feel like a dreamer,
I have dreams and goals,
Desires for a career, hopes for tomorrow.
And, in all of those you are my confidant.

You hear me say,
"I hope this for my family…"
Or, "I hope that for our future…"
And definitely, "I want this for my life"
And, God seldom do I truly pray for your will above mine.

I pray today about my dreams and my goals,
I pray for your will to be done.
Bring me to the place you want me to be,
Don't let my selfish desire distract me,
Teach me how to pray, "your will be done and not my own."

So, I can pray,
"Your will be done in my family…"
"Do as you will with my future…"
And definitely, "I want what your heart wills for my life."
God today I pray, in my dreams and my goals,
May your will be done.

Amen.

# Prayer for the Incarcerated

God of Liberty
We remember all those behind bars
And the families they've left behind.
You see purpose where others just see priors.
"Who the Son sets free, is free indeed!"
So break the bonds and let the captives go.

Jesus Christ, you too were falsely accused.
Son of God, you were also put in chains.
Apostles sang songs, and the cell doors swung wide,
So we cry out to you, God of the Exodus:
To break the chains of those incarcerated unjustly in our communities!

Thank you God, for wiping our record clean so we can start again.

Amen.

# Prayer When Our Faces Are Covered By Masks

God Our Keeper,
We know this season very well,
It has lasted quite some time,
Our faces are covered, and coverings are required,
Honestly, it is difficult to remember a time before masks.

We do this for protection,
We do this to take care
Of us and those we love.
We cover our faces and pray that you keep us safe,

Let us remember two things,
That even though our faces are covered,
Your face is always before us,
And that you are our ultimate protector.

In solidarity, guide us to care for our neighbor,
Maybe by covering our faces,
Or quickly showing them a smile.
Guide us to share your good news,
Though our faces might be covered.

Amen.

# Rejoicing in God's Justice

God: the maker of heaven and earth.
God: the maker of the sea and all that is in it.
God: who is faithful forever.
God: who gives justice to the oppressed.
God: who gives bread to the starving, but leaves the rich with an empty stomach.

The LORD: who frees prisoners.
The LORD: who makes the blind see.
The LORD: who straightens up those who are bent low.
The LORD: who loves the righteous.
The LORD: who protects immigrants, who helps orphans and widows, but who makes the way of the wicked twist and turn!

Praise the Lord, all who have breath,
Because of his righteousness and justice.
We lift up a shout because our God sees the little ones,
The left-out, and the lonely.
We trust that our God will bring about wholeness in our community,
And will include us in this holy work.

Amen.
From Psalms 146:6-9 CEB

# Prayer: When My body Doesn't Feel Like Home

Creator Of Every Body,
Thank you for making me in your image;
For numbering every hair on my head.
You say that you knit me together in the womb,
But I just don't feel at home.

You came to earth as a Human Body,
To a place that was not your home.
I know you know how it feels,
When I look at my skin,
The lumps and tissue, and think "Ew."

You see all of me;
Allow me to embrace myself as you do.
I surrender this feeling of loneliness over to you.
I name my discontent and discomfort before you.
Give me grace to find wholeness in you.

Amen.

# Prayer for Disappointment

Most High,
You command skies and seas.
Yet, you have been faithful to lil ole me.
You have given me all that I need, but I was hoping for _____.

I don't understand why this didn't work out;
It seemed like Your Will, as if it was meant to be.
I'm frustrated by circumstances, people, and even You.

I pray you would teach me to trust you and you alone.
I keep getting let down;
Don't let my anger get the best of me.

Give me a love for others that sees beyond their failures,
May I remember your grace is just as available to them as it is to me.
Allow me to rest and find contentment in the place that you have me.

Amen.

# Prayer Before a Loved One's Passing

God of all life,
Today I don't know how to pray,
I don't want _____ to pass away,
But, it seems to be time.

I pray for your mercy on _____,
If _____ knew you in this life,
I give you thanks,
Your child is going back to you,
If _____ did not know you on this side of eternity,
I pray that your grace is sufficient to cover for all things,

I pray for our family and friends,
All of those who will feel the emptiness after this loss,
Let your peace come upon us,
A realization beyond all understanding,
Telling us that you are in control and
Telling us that it is okay.

May we see the fullness of your grace,
Even through this,
May we see the greatness of your love,
At this moment, may your love overwhelm _____,
And please,
May your presence be felt even during our loss.

Amen.

# Prayer to Have The Posture of A Child at Play

God,
When praying, reading your word,
Or being with your people,

Let the posture of our hearts be
Like that of a child at play.

Like those who don't grow tired
Of living out their best adventure
Over and over again.

Amen.

Nadia
Volpini

# Oración Para Que Dios Nos Guíe a Amar

Señor,
Llévame a comenzar a amar,
Y a dejar de desechar.

Amen.

*Señor, llévame a comenzar a amar y a dejar de desechar. Amen*

*Nadia Volpini*

# Prayer for a Country Under Attack

Lord,
When we can't reach,
May you be reaching.

When we don't have words,
Be our prayers.

When we can't console,
May you be our peace.

When we can't help,
Be our response.

Be with our sisters and brothers,
In _____ (*add the country*)

Appear to them as you did that time,
With the disciples in that enclosed room.

Where there seemed to be no way in,
Nor a way out.

When you appeared,
And brought peace, life, and a future.

Please, remember your sons and daughters,
Our brothers and sisters, who you hold in your hands.

Amen.

# Prayer for the Death of an Unborn Child

God of all,

I did not get to meet this little one,
Yet I am struggling with the loss.

I have tried and tried to bring life,
Yet, all my efforts come up empty.

I did not know what to do,
And, I still don't know what to do.

You gave up your child for the greater good,
I felt I had to do the same.

So many lives are cut short,
I pray you would create more abundant life for us all.

You hold all of our sorrow and all of our hope together.
You carry the weight of what to do now and what to do next.

Restore life in our homes and our communities,
Bring hope and joy to those of us who have experienced loss.

Amen.

# Give us this day our daily bread

*And my God will meet all your needs according to the riches of his glory*
*in Christ Jesus.*
*Philippians 4:19*

# Prayer for a Meal

Bread of Life,
Thank you for knowing all our needs;
This food is a sign of your abundant gifts.
We can taste and see that you are good.
Thank you for giving us a planet that provides all we need.

Your table is a welcome place for all;
Help us to invite even our enemies to eat with us.
Transform foes into friends at this, your table.
We look forward to that big meal when you draw all the nations together.

We ask that every creature involved in this meal's creation gets fed too.
We pray that the hands that crafted it receive nourishment from you.
Use this meal to create unity, laughter, and strength.
Allow the energy to fuel your purpose in our lives.

In your name we pray,
Amen.

# A Prayer for Our Unexpected Sickness

Father,

I give you thanks for this body, the one that you have gifted me.
I thank you for all its parts, all its strengths,
All its members, and all its weaknesses.
Today, I am reminded of the frailty of my body.
It gets sick, and it hurts,
It gets weak and uncomfortable.

Healer,

I pray that you heal this body, the one that you have gifted me.
Even if complete healing will not come
Until that day when you come for all who are yours,
I do pray, please,
Heal this body.
Heal its frailty, by your love,
Cure its sickness, and appease its pain,
Empower its weakness, and bring comfort to it.

Lord,

I pray that you show your lordship over this body, the one that you have gifted me.
Please, empower me to still do your work
To live for your love, and live for your glory.
Today I am sick,
And I pray that you still use this sickened body
For your desire.
Father, Healer, Lord,
In your name, I pray,

Amen.

# A Prayer for Emptiness
### (Ezekiel 2:2)

Divine Spirit,

I don't know how to carry on.
Hold me together as I reach the end of my rope.
Fill this space with your presence as you fill all in all.

Draw me close when I'm feeling distant.
Help me resist turning to a temporary fix.
Lead me beyond myself.

Yes, God, you provide bread, rest, and strength for the journey.
Yes, Jesus, you hold all things together.
Yes, even in the beginning, Spirit, you hovered over dark, empty waters.

So Lord, lift me up, and set me on my feet once again.

Amen.

# Prayer after a COVID death

Jesus,
Who in all things became human,
I know that you are no stranger to this,
The pain, the suffering, the hurt,
The strange feeling of loss.
You are no stranger to death.

Today,
COVID-19 took someone I love.
And even when I am no stranger to loss,
Today feels different.
This hurts. And I need you.

Lord, pour your presence like ointment,
Here in my pain, amidst my loss,
Here on my wounds, when it hurts…
The hole left in our lives through this loss looms large
But remind me that your love can fill the empty space

I don't know all things, but,
One thing is for sure,
You are here,
Even amidst COVID-19,
You are here,
Mourning with me,

I am not alone,
Even today your voice is comforting me.
It might be difficult to hear, but please,
Give ears to my wounded heart,
I am listening.

Jesus, today your presence is with me,
Allow me to feel you,

Allow me to hear you,
Here next to me.

Amen.

# Prayer for Another Zoom Meeting

Creator of the Universe,
Beyond Space and Time,
Bring me into focus,
Help me to listen,
Let me speak with power and clarity.

Even though there's great distance between us
Here in this virtual space.
Be present to everyone on this call, even though I can't.
There is a time and season for all things;
Let us find purpose and wisdom, we know you can.

Amen.

# Thanksgiving for a Meal

God, our provider,
We give you thanks for this food,
We thank you because once, and once again,
You provide for us,
And, you provide for those we love,

We pray for those who feel forgotten at this very moment,
We pray for those who do not have a similar meal before them,
We pray that you show yourself faithful to them,
Just as you are faithful to us.

We pray that you use us to provide for those who feel discarded,
We pray, please use us to give them food,
That their plates may be overflowing with love,
So that as they taste your provision, we might be an extension of your love.

We pray so that just as we are giving thanks,
That soon those who feel forgotten can also give thanks,
That you move us to show your faithfulness,
So that we all, us and those who feel forgotten, can rejoice in your provision.

Amen.

# Prayer for Rest

Jesus,
You teach us to rest
To sleep through storms and run from busyness
You remind us that humans were not made for Sabbath
But Sabbath, you made for us
We welcome the rest you provide for us

Father,
In the desert, you taught us to trust you for each meal
That every good and perfect thing comes from you
Thank you that you don't measure my worth by productivity
Let my hands come to a halt & my feet to settle

Spirit,
Thank you for comforting and guiding us through everything
You empower us for work and prepare us for relaxation
Remind me of my smallness and fragility
Release me from anxiety and give me peace

Amen.

# Prayer on the Verge of a Monetary Gift

Blessed Lord,
On the verge of another monetary gift,
Please remind us that everything belongs to you.

Even what is gifted to us,
All of it is ultimately yours.

Remind us to be good stewards of your gifts,
And, please, use us to bless those in need
Of your monetary graces.

Amen.

# A Prayer against Shame

Jesus,

On open wounds, you were spit on by those who hated you.
You felt the judgment of your fellows.
You carried the weight of guilt, despite your innocence.

I feel sick with shame.
I feel the judgment of others and myself.
I feel _____.

Help me to lift my face in confidence,
Knowing that you have made me new.
Give me peace while I take blow after blow.

I pray for strength to carry out your will.
Allow me to let go of everything else.
Thank you for freeing me from shame and giving me salvation.

Amen.

# And forgive us our trespasses as we forgive those who trespass against us;

*Above all, maintain constant love for one another,
for love covers a multitude of sins.
1st Peter 4:8*

*Therefore confess your sins to one another, and pray for one another, so that
you may be healed. The prayer of the righteous is powerful and effective.
James 5:16*

# A Prayer for Strangers You Meet Today

God of all Creation,

Lift up the stranger that I will pass on the sidewalk,
At work, at Walmart.

Would you give peace to each one,
Be with their concerns and fears.

Would you give me eyes to see deeply,
Patience with all creation as I move about.

Knowing that your purpose weaves all of life together,
Allow me to see you in the beings I bump into today.

Amen.

# Relating with God Amidst Busyness

## (Reflecting on John 6:11)

Father,
Today will be busy, as many other days, maybe even more.
I want to be the best in all things,
With my studies, my responsibilities at work,
My roles at home, my time to serve,
and my time to rest,
but time and time again I find myself failing.
Perhaps at one of these tasks, if not all at once.

Today, remind me of your presence,
Pull me closer to you.
Remind me that at your pastures,
While listening to your voice,
When I am in need of you,
It's there where you distribute the loaves and the fish.
And not just some,
But as much as I need.

Father, today will be busy,
But I pray, bring me to a stillness today,
So I can be with you,
And be fed by the provision of your presence.

Amen.

## TO DO:

1) Read Bible
2) Get Ready for the day
3) Drive to work
4) Complete task 1
5) Complete task 2
6) Complete task 3
7) Lunch
8) Complete task 4
9) Complete task 5
10) Complete task 6
11) Drive home
12) Go to Gym
13) Cook dinner
14) Spend time with family
15) Watch tv / Relax
16) Get ready for bed
17) Repeat again tomorrow

God's to do list for me:

## BE STILL

<sup>13</sup> Know that I am GOD.

— Psalm 46:10

Nadia Volpini

# A Prayer for Racial Reconciliation
## (White Man's Perspective)

God, I come with a heavy heart.
Knowing countless times we have had Your Name in our mouths on Sunday,
Unwilling to say the name of a Black woman or man on Monday.
Immeasurable violence done by praying hands right after church.

My sister and I stand oceans apart,
Because of the oceans their ancestors were dragged across by mine.
My brother lives with a fear I will never know,
With painful memories and trauma I cannot behold.

We have heard evil on the lips of our loved ones,
And we said nothing.
We have seen neglect, mistreatment, and violence,
And we turned a blind eye.

Give us ears to listen and new eyes to see oppression.
Give us the courage to confess our brokenness and call out injustice.
Give us your love to forge authentic relationships and hold honest conversation.
So That All the Children of God Can Say Together,

Amen!

# Prayer For Racial Reconciliation
## (From a Black Latino Man)

Jesus,
I have lived it, I have felt it,
The difference that race makes,
The weight of the powers of sin and death,
Pushing me down because of the color my skin,
Because of the language I speak.

And, amidst it all, I have seen you,
My ever present help,
I have lived amidst the love of your church,
I have seen how your body brings life to my body,
And how the color of my skin matters,
And the language I speak also does.

But, beyond both of those,
Your sacrifice at the cross matters the most.
Yes, that sacrifice so that your people may be one,
As you and your Father and the Spirit are one.
So, today I pray in two ways,

First, I give you thanks,
Thanks for who you made me to be,
Thanks for the color of this skin,
Thanks for this language I speak,
Thanks for the weight that is on me,
Because I know I don't carry it alone,
You and your church carry it with me,
And, weight training together, just makes us stronger, together.

Second, I forgive, as you taught us to forgive,
Just as your prayer says,
I forgive those who have trespassed against us,

Those who sold my ancestors back in Africa,
I forgive them,
Those who enslaved my ancestors in the Americas,
I forgive them,
And, those who still live under the oppression of racism,
I forgive them.

And, Jesus,
I pray you forgive them too.
I pray that your love will make them new, too.
I pray that all our generations will look more like you too,
That your Holy Body is made one as the Trinity is one too,
And that your people will be reconciled to each other,
As we seek to be reconciled to you too.

For your glory, and in your name I pray,

Amen.

# Prayer Before Watching Porn

Creator of this body,
I have been affected by images from the past,
I have been influenced by my culture,
And thoughts of improper sex appear in my mind,
God, in this state,
And with temptation at hand,
I pray to you, please, strengthen me to not watch porn.

I pray to you,

God of my sexuality,
Remind me of the pain that comes from pornography,
The misuse of the body,
The participants, people indeed,
But made into objects of a scene.
The systems of corruption a part of the sex industry,
The stories of rape, abuse, deceit, mistreat,
And, the story of so many whose bodies have been trafficked for it.

I pray to you,

God of all truth,
Remind me of the lies involved with pornography,
The deceit of performed sexuality,
The lie that one partner is not enough,
The lie that virtual sex,
Is better than personal intimacy.
The lie that pleasure is the aftermath of watching porn,
When, instead, the aftermath is the awareness of the emptiness in me.

Please, I pray to you,

God of abundant life,
Remind me that I need satisfaction,
And remind me that only you

Will ever be enough for me.
Pornography will never suffice,
*But you alone can satisfy.*
You alone can bring fullness to this life,
And you alone can truly fill this heart.

Bring your strength to the weakness in me,
So I will not watch pornography,
So my eyes will be fixed on you.
My Creator, my God...my Help,
In your name, and for your glory I pray,
Amen.

# Prayer for loving those
## Of different political party

Jesus, our beloved friend,
Teach us to love our neighbor,
Even beyond their political affiliation,
Even beyond their beliefs about abortion or gender relations,
Even beyond their understanding of racial reconciliation,
Even when they don't care about these issues.

Please, teach us to love our neighbor,
Move our hearts to be closer to yours,
That we can give our lives for those
Who think differently from us,
Help us show the world we are your disciples,
So all can see our witness because of the way we love.

In your love and for your witness we pray,

Amen.

# Prayer: Confession of Doubt

God,
We speak to you every day,
Sometimes formally,
By written and solemn prayers,
Other times simply by a passing comment.

But God, even then,
Even when we speak to you,
We doubt.
We confess it,
We have a doubting heart.

We doubt your existence,
We doubt that you listen,
We doubt your grace to save,
And your power to heal.
We doubt you.

We doubt your work in our life,
We doubt that you are still working in the world,
We doubt that you gave us a purpose, and
Though the scripture says you do,
We doubt that you love us.

God,
We confess our doubting heart,
And we pray that you listen to our confession,
And we pray that you show us you are here, with us,
Please, show us that you love us.
So as of today, we won't doubt.

Amen.

# Prayer: Confession of Judgmental Thoughts

God,

I often find myself thinking I'm better than others.
I scroll past a post and think "how stupid!"
I judge someone's choice of clothing.
I roll my eyes when I hear people speak from their heart.
I have labeled and stereotyped people.
I have been looking down on folks made in your image.

I confess, I haven't been humble enough to see my own double standards.
Lord, I have been busy picking at others,
Instead of picking up your work of love and peace.
Give me eyes to see people as you do.
Allow me to have compassion and empathy for all people.
Help my passion to lead me to humility.

Amen.

# Prayer: Confession of Selfishness

God my Provider,
I know that I can ask for anything I need.
In a world where so many have so little,
you have given me more than enough;
But I've been caught up chasing more lately.
I want more out of my relationships.
No matter what I buy, it's not enough.
Caught up in my busyness, I don't have time for You.

I confess, I've been selfish with my time, relationships, and money.
I find myself longing for more attention and affirmation.
Give me contentment in what I have.
Help me find joy in the relationships and the work right in front of me.
Rid me of selfishness.
Help me make a world where your gifts are not hoarded but shared.

Amen.

# Prayer: Confession of sin against a brother/sister

God,
I confess that I have sinned.

I have sinned against you God almighty,
Loving Father, Great Provider, Creator of all.

And I have sinned against your people,
I have wronged my sisters and brothers.

Please, as you have done before,
Forgive my sin once again.

Take me by the hand,
And lead me beyond today,

For those I've hurt, those who my selfishness wronged,
I pray that you heal.

And, though I don't deserve it,
I ask that they might forgive me.

God, I confess that I've sinned,
I pray for your forgiving embrace to surround me.

Amen.

# Prayer When Experiencing Anger

God of Wrath,
I come to you with my fists clenched.
My heart burns with rage.
Questions like "how could they do this?" swirl in my mind;
Followed by "how could you let this happen?"

I can't put to words the frustration I feel.
I'm exhausted by how many times I've heard cheap apologies;
I've been brushed off and dismissed.
But you won't ignore my cries of anguish.

God of Justice,
In my anger, don't let me sin.
We follow your son, teacher who turned tables in the Temple;
But also told Peter to put down the sword.

Provide an outlet for my anger;
One that is not sinful, one that reflects you.
Allow me to find a just cause to stand behind.
Don't let me pass on the harm that I've experienced.
By your power, help me transform my anger into righteous action.

Amen.

# Prayer Before Filing For Divorce

My Beloved,
I am tired,
I am weak,
The pain is so repetitive,
I am hurting over and over,
It's always the same thing.

I want to leave my spouse,
And maybe try again,
Our relationship is not working,
And none of us is trying anymore.
At this point, we are only hurting each other.

I do want to file for divorce,
That might be a good option.
But, Beloved,
Time and time again,
I am reminded of your love.

The love that has forgiven me,
Once, twice, and thrice,
And so many more times.
Your love for someone like me,
With my faults and imperfections.

Your love that grew tired,
Weak, hurting, and in pain on that cross.
Your love that saw me truly, but never left,
And though our relationship wasn't working,
You kept on trying, you never gave up.

My Beloved Jesus, I pray,
Please, help my marriage.
May your love fill me everyday,

May your love fill my spouse every day,
And may we love each other because of You.

May we empty ourselves for each other,
Respect each other's love,
Stop hurting one another,
And not give up on what you established,
That no-one and no-thing could separate us.

I want to file for divorce,
But please, work in,
And transform my heart.
Also please, work in,
And transform my spouse's heart.

For your glory,
God of all love,
Who never gave up on me
My Beloved Jesus,
In your name, I pray,

Amen.

*(If you or someone that you know is experiencing sexual, physical, mental, or emotional abuse please reach out to someone that can help. Domestic Violence Hotline: 800.799. 7233)*

# Petición: Recordatorio de la Gracia de Dios

Señor,
Recuerdame de tu gracia por mí.

Y fortaléceme para mostrar tu gracia
A aquellos que han herido mi corazón.

Amen.

# Prayer for The Immigrant

God of all creation,
You love all of us,
You love us greatly,
So much that you gave your life, for us.

We pray for those who have had to emigrate,
For those whose lives have changed,
To where they can only see one option:
To leave, to escape, to let go of what they have known.

We pray for those who are stuck in borders,
Those who are without,
Without food, without a home,
Without security, without a future.

We pray that you show yourself as all they need,
Their Father, their Provider,
Their Security, Their Home,
Their Future.

We pray that you help us understand them,
That we don't simply categorize them as "immigrants,"
But that we see them as your creation,
Who you love greatly, for whom you died.

We pray that we learn to embrace them,
And their experience, their loneliness,
Their hurt, their insecurity, their trauma,
And their need for you.

We pray for all the immigrants,
Those coming to this country,
And those who go to others,
Lord, be with them.

And be with us,
As we learn to love them dearly,
Just as you have loved us,
Just as you love them.

Amen.

# Prayer When Wanting to Be "Desired" by Someone Other Than My Spouse/Partner/Honey

Beloved Jesus,
I am in a relationship,
With someone I love,
But I am not seen,
And, I don't feel wanted,
Nor appreciated, or loved.

Others appear to see me,
They seem to notice me,
And I want to be with them,
I want to be desired,
I want to be wanted.

In my want, oh Jesus, I pray,
Please bring me back the memory,
The reminder of your cross,
The moment when *you* saw *me*.
When *you* showed that *you* love *me*.

You appreciate me,
You want me,
You desire to be with me.
You care for me,
You love me.

Bring to my memory your faithfulness,
So, even though I don't feel seen,
Because you were faithful to me,
I can be faithful to whom I am with.

In the relationship I am in.

I pray, Beloved,
Fill this relationship with your love,
That we can be faithful to each other,
So we can see, want, appreciate, desire,
And love each other, as you love us.

My Beloved Jesus,
I give this relationship to you,
Please, overwhelm us both with your love,
So we may love each other more,
More like you do.

Amen.

# And lead us not into temptation, but deliver us from evil.

*Submit yourselves, then, to God.*
*Resist the devil, and he will flee from you.*
*James 4:7*

# Prayer for Arguments on Social Media
## (Reflections on James 1)

Alpha and Omega
You are present to our circumstances.
You see all my thoughts
You hear the longing of my heart.
I thank you for the passion you've placed in me;
May it be matched by your compassion.

Remind us of the scriptures that say,
"Blessed are the peacemakers," in the same breath as
"Let justice roll down like a mighty river."
May this conversation sharpen and build up,
Rather than tear us down.

Give us humility,
Let me be quick to listen,
Slow to speak,
Slow to become angry.

Remind us of our smallness, our fragility,
We see only in a dim mirror, but soon we will see face to face.
Let me log off and exit out,
Let my heart be at rest,
That I may be more attentive to your Spirit.

Amen.

# Prayer for Peace in the Church

Lord,
In the past we have faced the powers,
The work of the evil one among your people,
And, today we are facing them again,
The evil one is trying to destroy your work.

We see those among us who have in mind
Things of the world and not of you,
Those among us who are opposed to your loving work,
Those among us who refuse to enter into conversation,
Those among us who are acting against the peace of your Spirit.

Once again we see the powers moving,
We see the evil one acting,
And your people are being influenced by evil.

But, we remember your word and your power,
We know the power of your name, Jesus,
The redemption of your love,
The healing of your grace,
And the authority of your thunderous voice.

So in your name we pray,
A rebuke on the evil one,
A rebuke upon the powers of evil,
A rebuke of your people,
And, the restoration of your Spirit in your church.

We desire you over all other things,
And, we believe in your work among us today.
Jesus in your name, in your authority, and for your glory,
We pray, let it be so,

Amen.

# A Prayer Against Algorithms

Father God,
Thank you for giving us the strength to stand
against all the temptations of the evil one!
We confess that we are prone to wander,
Prone to consume rather than connect.

All day, we receive lies rather than truth.
Every indulgence and outrage is at our fingertips .
Advertisements sell us every appearance,
But, remind us that we are made in your loving image.

We rebuke the algorithms that feed our worst fears.
We flee from the urges to click and share and scroll.
In the name of Jesus, we tear down strongholds of lust and luxury,
Because the powers of evil are no match for your peace.

We ask that you please deliver us from evil.
Our desires conspire against your purposes.
Give us the strength to put down our devices,
And surrender to You.

Amen.

# Not Against Flesh
## (Reflection on Ephesians 6:10-17)

Lord,
We have heard it said over and over again,
"For our struggle is not against flesh and blood"
But we seldom know what it means to,
"Put on the whole armor of God."

God, we pray,
Give us eyes to see the work of evil,
Give us hearts to discern between flesh, blood,
and the powers of darkness,

Teach us that the corruption,
The deceit and egocentric focus of our governments,
Is just an example of the influence
That belongs to the rulers of evil.

Teach us that evil is still at work,
Among our fellow students, our workmates,
Our friends, our partners, our family,
And, even *in* us.

Today, we clothe ourselves with your armor,
And we take our stand against the devil's schemes.
With your truth, your justice, your peace,
Your faithfulness, your salvation,
And your living Word who is *in* us.

For your glory, and your name,
Amen.

# Prayer of Resistance

Jesus the Liberator,
Even though the evil one comes only to steal, kill, & destroy,
We thank you for giving us abundant life.
In your name, by your blood, we will overcome

Jesus, in your name, we rebuke those who steal the land,
Those who steal wages,
Those who steal dignity and joy with words and deeds.
Help us to resist "The Thief" in our lives.

We rebuke those that take life,
Those who prey on the innocent,
Those of us who celebrate the death of our enemies.
Help us to resist the devil's war on life.

We rebuke addictions that destroy families and friendship,
The corporations that destroy God's Creation,
Those abusers who wreck homes and scar bodies.
Help us to resist the Destroyer by building your Kingdom.

God, we need your healing in the midst of violence.
We need your restoration where there is brokenness.
Empower us to tear down every stronghold of the enemy,
And, let us be relentless in our resistance to evil.

Amen.

# Prayer to Lift Our Thoughts to God

Holy One,
I lift up my thoughts to you.

I am distracted easily,
Please, keep my mind focused on you.

I am lusting and objectifying others,
Please, guide my desires.

I am thinking of self harm,
Please, let me know my worth.

I am hateful and prejudiced against others,
Please, remind me of their worth.

My thoughts are selfish and prideful,
Please humble me.

I am dwelling on lies about myself,
Please, reveal your truth to me.

I ask for strength to resist the devil,
I rebuke any thoughts that set themselves up against your will.

Amen.

# Prayer for Someone Who is Demon Possessed

Jesus,
We call on your name **Jesus**,
For in us there is not enough strength,
For even the archangel Gabriel wasn't strong enough,
To rebuke the devil,
When he was disputing for Moses' body,

So **Jesus**, in your name,
We rebuke the devil,
We your church rebuke the power of evil,
We rebuke the demonic influence on _____,
And we pray that it is gone from _____,

And we declare an infilling of your Spirit,
We pray that _____ is filled by your Holy Spirit
Just as you infill your people with your Spirit,
We proclaim, in word and deed,
That _____ is not taken by demonic powers anymore,
And that now _____ is filled by your breath of life.

We rebuke the false identity, the demonic identity,
That inhabited the life of _____,
And we declare the truth of who _____ is in you,
_____ is your child, adopted by your love, transformed by your grace,
Redeemed by your sacrifice, and restored by your life.

**Jesus**, we give _____ to you,
_____ is yours and yours alone,
In your name,

Amen.

# Prayer of Protection
## (Deuteronomy 32:11-12; Exodus 19:1-6; Psalm 91)

Father God,
Thank you for bringing us this far,
For going the hard way before us.
Guide us every step we take, every place we visit.
Give us wisdom in all our decisions.
We pray against any force sent to do us harm.

Mother Eagle,
Hide us in the shadow of your wings.
Protect us from evil and help us stand against the enemy.
Help us take refuge in your power.
Secure our families and our future.
Allow us to walk the narrow path that leads to life.

Amen.

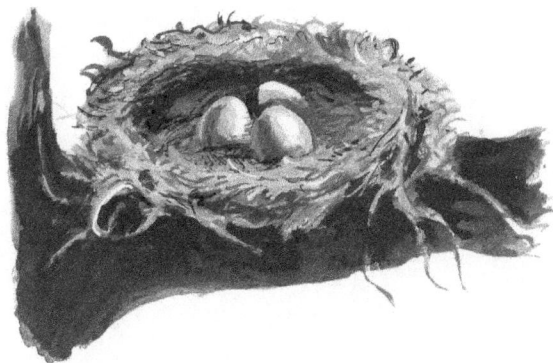

# For yours is the kingdom, the power and the glory forever. Amen.

*For who is God except the Lord? Who but our God is a solid rock? God is my strong fortress, and he makes my way perfect.*
*2 Samuel 22:33*

# Prayer for Gratitude
## (When I am not grateful)

God,
Today I struggle being grateful
I don't know what to say,
I don't know how to give thanks,
But, I know in my deepest being,
I know you deserve my gratefulness,

God,
Help me to be grateful for today,
Give me eyes to see your beauty,
Give me ears to hear your loving words,
Give me words to give you thanks,
Please, give me a grateful heart,

God, today I say to you "Thanks!"
Amen.

# Prayer of Praise

Praised be you,
My God, My Friend,
You are always present, even when we've tried to push you away,

Praised be you,
My Father and Creator,
Since the beginning you have cared for us, your people.

Praised be you,
My Lord, my King,
You have ruled your creation and shown your love at every moment.

Praised be you,
My Savior, my Beloved,
Your love has changed us forever.

Praised be you,
My Breath, my Mother,
You have been with us in all this journey,

Praised be you,
My Guide, My Counselor,
Without you our lives would not be the same.

Praised be you, God,
Father, Son, and Spirit,
You deserve all our praise, throughout all our days,

Amen.

Nadra
Volpini

# Acknowledgments

Ashton S. Dupler:

First and foremost, I would like to thank my God, Creator of the Universe and also the savior of my soul. My family, who gave me the foundation for these prayers and who taught me how to pray. My wife, Kasey, who always finds a way to remind me and even physically make me sit down and pray when I need it most. To my mentors in the faith, and especially London Coe and Pastor Peter Matthews; I would not have written this without your guidance. To my fellow congregants and colleagues at McKinley United Methodist Church and the Dayton Equity Center, God used you all to save me, I am forever grateful. To those friends who have held space for me and prayed for me in many different forms, thank you for everything. To those churches and universities, thank you for pushing me forward in my faith and hopeful in my pursuit of justice.

Edward K. Solano Johnson:

I would like to thank my wife Ashley for always inspiring me to try new and creative avenues of expression. Without her this work would not have been possible. Right alongside her, I want to thank my parents and sister: Cruz Solano (dad), Sara Johnson (mom), and Sarah Solano Johnson (sister). God placed me in a loving family that supports my endeavors wholeheartedly. Their love and investment in my life is invaluable. I also want to thank some of my mentors, professors, and guides in this season of life: Jim Singletary, Lincoln Stevens, Jeanne Serrão, Mark Ledford, Joseph Ford, and Eric Vail. Their intellectual and spiritual guidance allowed me to seek the Lord more faithfully, and to pray more honest and vulnerable prayers. I thank my brothers and sisters from the Westerville Church of the Nazarene for their support and love, my church family from the Dios Es Suficiente Iglesia del Nazareno, and so many other friends that have become like family. Over all things, I am grateful to God for the love, care, gifts, and graces extended to me. Without God I could do nothing, nor would I want to do anything. To God be the glory.

# About the Authors

## Ashton S. Dupler

Ashton moved from his hometown in rural Ohio to innercity Dayton after graduating with a degree in Urban Ministry from Mount Vernon Nazarene University. He serves as Associate Pastor of Historic McKinley United Methodist Church (UMC) alongside St. Paul UMC. With a passion for justice issues, Ashton serves as Associate Director of the Dayton Equity Center, to create initiatives that restore communities alongside congregations.

With years of experience in logistics and manufacturing, Ashton Dupler has been the primary instigator behind new workforce initiatives for people with language, cultural, and criminal barriers to employment. He and his wife, Kasey, live with their dog in Dayton and can be found outside of work hiking, disc golfing, and trying new restaurants. Ashton has a Master of Divinity from Methodist Theological School in Ohio. In preparation for an upcoming podcast, you can follow him on Instagram @ashtondupler33

# Edward K. Solano Johnson

Edward is originally from Honduras in Central America. Currently, he and his wife Ashley live in Columbus, Ohio. Edward enjoys hiking, playing music, meeting new people, a good match of table tennis or chess, and experiencing new cultures.

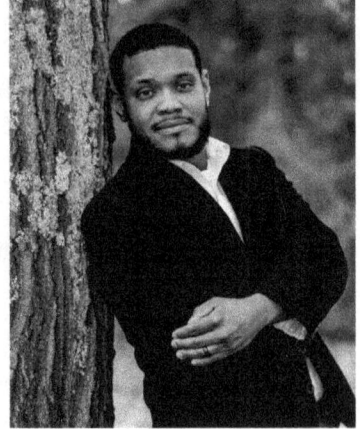

His creative thought has been heavily influenced by a variety of people: Spiritual writers like Henri Nouwen and Howard Thurman. Philosophers and theologians like Søren Kierkegaard and Jürgen Moltmann. And poets like Pablo Neruda, Sor Juana Ines de la Cruz, and Rudy Francisco.

In 2022, Edward and Ashley hiked the Camino Primitivo of El Camino de Santiago, a pilgrimage in northern Spain. Edward considered this experience to be deeply profound. Through being a pilgrim he understood deeply rooted truths about God's love for all people. He says that, "God seeks to find us in every section of our life's path. As we continue walking through life, instant by instant we are guided to a deeper realization of God's divine love." If you are interested in hearing more from Edward you can follow him on Instagram: @urblacktinofriend

# About the Illustrators

## Nadia Volpini

Nadia Volpini is an illustrator based in Columbus Ohio. As a child she was always doing arts and crafts, which has stuck with her into adulthood. She got great practice and explored multiple mediums in high school art classes which she was always taking. Since then, she mainly works on art projects in her downtime. She enjoys drawing, painting, collaging, scrapbooking, working with air clay, DIY projects, and is still exploring more mediums. Her other passions include reading, knitting, learning new languages, trying new sports, and organizing her Pinterest boards

## Edward Steffanni

Edward Steffanni is an American artist born in Ohio. He received his Master of Fine Arts in Printmaking from the Rhode Island School of Design.

Edward is an interdisciplinary artist using primarily print, paint and performance to explore subjects familiar to his Middle American upbringing, examining the relationships between sexuality, community, and spirituality. His work has been exhibited nationally and has received awards within those exhibitions. Most recently, he was a recipient of the prestigious Elizabeth Greenshields Foundation grant. His work is held in the collection of the University of Richmond Museums, among others. He currently teaches at University of Toledo among other academic institutions. For more on his works, visit edwardsteffanni.com

## SCAN ME!

TO SIGN UP FOR STORIES FROM THE FORGE

@DSMSTORYFORGE // DSMSTORYFORGE.COM